A HARVEST OF MEMORIES

A HARVEST OF MEMORIES

A Wartime Evacuee in Kent

Gina Hughes

Book Guild Publishing
Sussex, England

First published in Great Britain in 2005 by
The Book Guild Ltd
25 High Street
Lewes, East Sussex
BN7 2LU

Typesetting in Times by
SetSystems Ltd, Saffron Walden, Essex

Printed in Great Britain by
CPI Bath

A catalogue record for this book is
available from the British Library

ISBN 1 85776 981 3

1

On 1st September 1939 I was evacuated with the girls of Downham Central School, Bromley, Kent to an unknown destination as war seemed imminent. I was eleven years old and had been at my new school only a few months having left Rangefield Road Downham Junior School. My parents had spoken of my brother Ivon, five years my senior, and I going out to Australia to stay with our Auntie Alice, Mum's sister, for the duration of the war but they decided against this.

So we boarded a train and were taken to Headcorn in Kent. We travelled with a light luggage of clothing, gas mask and emergency rations and we had a postcard which was pre-addressed and stamped to write to our parents telling them of our safe arrival and our billet address. None of us realized what it was all about and just enjoyed looking out of the carriage window. Perhaps the older children and the few parental helpers, and of course our teachers, were very apprehensive!

From Headcorn we were taken to Biddenden, a journey of approximately 5 miles by coach, and then into the village hall. Quite a few people were waiting for us to arrive and soon they were picking out the number of children they could accommodate. A girl named Rita Rowland and myself were asked to go with a lady and were driven away 2½ miles to our billet. Rita's mother came as a helper so had to stay with the children and our teachers in the village hall until they were settled, and she herself would not be billeted with her daughter. Rita and I were taken to a large house and the lady returned to her car.

'Oh,' I thought, 'she isn't going to be looking after us. Pity, as she seemed very nice'. We were taken into the house by a lady who told us her name was Floss and that we were to meet her uncle named Mr Walter Bingham, and that she helped run the house for him. Floss seemed a very nice kind lady and was quite young, about 26. Mr Bingham sat on a long sofa with just one end to it which was covered with a rough brown blanket, and a black spaniel dog sat beside him. There was a large table in the middle of the room and dining chairs, corner cupboards and a large bureau and brass candle sticks on the mantle piece and some brass saucepans shone brightly on top of the corner cupboard, plus a huge grandfather clock stood in the corner of the room.

Mr Bingham smiled at us and his blue eyes twinkled. He had rosy cheeks and one large 'winkle picker' of a tooth jutted out over his bottom lip. He was surprised that Rita and I hadn't got a broad Cockney accent since we lived on the outskirts of London. He was even more surprised and Floss too, that we enjoyed ordinary food and not just fish and chips and beer which they were led to believe about us. We handed over our emergency rations, but were too tired to eat and were asked if we would like a drink of milk or ginger beer! I settled for milk, Rita didn't want anything but was puzzled about the ginger beer.

Soon we were off to bed with a promise to show us around in the morning – it had been quite a day. More

2

surprises were in store when we saw our large four-poster bed. We were told not to jump about on it – the decorative knobs on the top might fall off! It was a feather bed, very cosy, and made a nest around us. We also had a chamber pot for our use.

I don't know who woke up first in the night, Rita or I, but it was the moonlight which shone into the room through the partially drawn curtains that awoke us, making strange shadows on the walls. Most eerie though was the even stranger sound of a sighing and breathing which hauntingly came nearer and nearer in our fertile imagination.

'Call Floss,' I said in a giant whisper.

Floss came looking like the ghost itself, dressed in a long white nightie and her face distorted from the flickering candle she held high and us only daring to peep over the top of the sheets. We told her our fears and she kindly drew the curtains closer and then listened to the strange noise.

'Why, that's only the dog. She sleeps on Uncle's bed. Nothing to be afraid of. Would you like a drink of ginger beer?' We politely declined and were soon off to sleep.

In the morning we were called down to the kitchen and the first rule laid down was that once downstairs we stayed down – we were not to keep running up and down. At the bottom of the stairs, and opposite the sitting/dining room we'd been in on arrival, was the parlour. We were allowed to look in but as it was only used occasionally it was out of bounds to us. It did look very nice and had a piano and pretty chairs and ornaments, and lots of nice things that I can't remember.

In a large passageway doors went off to a dairy, a walk-in larder, and a cellar, from which I saw Mr Bingham appear that evening with a small jug containing

3

his good strong best cider, only given to chosen friends. It could rot your socks, it was so powerful.

Near to the front door, which was never used, stood a tall cupboard in which Mr Bingham stored his guns – never, ever, were we to touch that cupboard or its guns.

Back down the passage and near to the cellar door was a large kitchen with a red brick floor and a very big, rather shallow, red brick sink and along one narrow end stood a pump with a long handle. Floss told us that it pumped pond water from a nearby pond and was their water supply. If this got low they fetched it by pails from other ponds which were further away. So no mains water.

There was another door at the back of the kitchen which led on to a back staircase to one of the five bedrooms but had been sealed off for many years. Soon we noticed the black solid-fuel stove on which stood a huge brown kettle, gently boiling. A brass primus stove stood close to the sink and Floss picked up a floor-size scrubbing brush to wash some bits of food down to the plug hole. Various candle holders, with remains of used candles, were scattered on tops of cupboards. I remembered that Floss had told us not to touch the oil lamp on the dining table. I realised that the house had no electricity or gas.

The kitchen table held an assortment of breakfast dishes with cereals, pots of jam and a very large dish with cheese, and plates of eggs and bacon. Uncle had had his breakfast and was out milking, and Floss said she would take us out when she fed the chickens after we'd had ours. We were given tea to drink which looked rather black, but were told we could drink as much milk as we liked as we couldn't drink the water, only when boiled as in tea. Now I understood – homemade ginger beer (water was boiled and the ginger disguised the otherwise nasty flavour) or milk to drink.

Oh wonder of wonders, I realised for the first time that we were on a farm. I adored animals, and at home we only had our very dear black cat. I did ask for a pony one Christmas but got a three-wheeled bike instead, which made me cry! But of course it was out of the question both financially and practically.

I spotted a small comfortable type of armchair covered in a coarse floral material near to the warm stove and sat down in it, and was hastily but kindly told, 'That's Jill's chair. She is the only one to use it, as it's her chair.'

Who was Jill? I wondered, but not for long, as Mr Bingham and the spaniel came back from milking. He had a large harness on his shoulders and suspended from it with heavy chains were pails of milk. The harness, I was to learn, was called a yoke. The spaniel's name was Jill. Mr Bingham was wearing a cap and round his waist tied with string was a hessian sack. His cap remained on all day, only revealing the pale forehead line above his ruddy complexion when work was done for the day. We were soon to learn that other than necessary farm work, no sewing, knitting, darning and so on was done on the Sabbath. There was no TV of course, or even a wireless of any sort, and Mr Bingham was the only one to read the newspaper, which was during the evening. There were plenty of conversations on farm matters, and also about the war, which hadn't been declared yet. Floss asked if Rita and I would get our stamped addressed postcards and she told us the farm's address which was East Ongley Farm, Biddenden, Kent. The postman would be coming soon and collected mail for posting as well as delivering it.

5

Soon we were out in the fields where we saw sheep, cows, hens, pigs, geese and a huge, beautiful grey and white dappled horse called Boxer. He had long white hair hanging over his hooves and was quite fat with a broad back. I think he was a Shire horse, and he and I were to become close friends. I would talk to him about everything and I'm sure he liked that, especially in the summer when the flies bothered him, and I gently brushed them away from his eyes. I learned to recognise a horsefly too which can distress a horse so much as it has a long stinging probe, and I would give it an almighty swipe in case it got me too.

The fields had names like Little Batchelor, Little Ongley and Five Acres, according to size. The farm was 75 acres and they grew hops and had an oast house in which to dry them. More about that later. Around the oast house were various barns, cowsheds, pig pens, calf enclosures and dung heaps. Feral cats lived there, who were given milk but had to catch the mice and rats for their food. Mr Bingham was very kind to them and did give them titbits from time to time. This whole area was called The Buildings. There were beehives in front of the farmhouse and several apple trees, from one of which we were told we could eat as many apples as we liked. They were small but delicious. Opposite the farm kitchen door was a building called The Lodge in which they kept huge barrels and bins of feed for the hens and meal for calves, also logs for the stove and general fire purposes indoors and out.

Of course mice and rats liked The Lodge too! I was to be accustomed to these as one had to go through there to the 'bog' which consisted of a wooden two-hole toilet seat, one hole larger than the other, side by side, and just earth beneath. Paper torn up into squares from an old farm catalogue threaded onto string hung

6

on the whitewashed wall. At the bottom where the toilet was boxed in, in the right-hand corner of this was a small hole. I was later to see many a rat's tail disappearing down this hole and so I used to rattle the door catch loudly on entering to frighten them away. I always used the small hole – I thought it was safer! I must add here that Floss's sister Grace once came screaming out of the lodge with her knickers round her ankles. 'Uncle' (Mr Bingham) got his gun and, standing at the kitchen door, shot the rat who was still in sight.

Once a small animal was seen in the same area a couple of times and as they didn't know what it was, having had only a glimpse, the animal was trapped the same as some of the rats. I remember they were very upset when they found it was an otter which they said was a rare animal. They didn't let me see it, as it was dead.

We used a candle to light the toilet, but often when it was moonlight relieving oneself under the leaning, very old Bramley apple trees besides the house was permissible, although the nearby cabbage patch was definitely out of bounds! The contents of the toilet were dug out every so often and taken somewhere on the land, usually when I was at school.

The next day Sunday Rita and I were taken across the fields on some of the public footpaths which crossed East Ongley Farm and other neighbouring farms to Biddenden Church. It only took 20 or 25 minutes, compared to the 2½-mile walk round the lane and road to the village. A lady social worker had come by the previous day to see if we were settling into our billet, which we were, but Rita was already missing her mother, knowing she was billeted in the village. So near but so far! Also, where? The lady had told Floss we had to attend the church service and to start school

7

on Monday, where we would share the village school by going in the mornings only. I was used to attending church at home as we had one opposite our house, on the large council estate that my parents had lived in since it was first built.

Half-way through the service a man walked up to the rector, looking very serious, and handed him a written note. The rector went up into the pulpit and solemnly declared that we were now at war with Germany. I immediately thought that we must be careful when we walked back to the farm because there would be Germans in the ditches with guns. I was very pleased when everything seemed just the same as when we had come to church. It was all very puzzling.

We started going to the local village school in the mornings and the local children attended in the afternoons. One day, whilst in the school playing field, which faced the church, Rita and I saw Mr Bingham, Floss, Frank and a few other people coming out of the church entrance. As it was a week day I was surprised, and said to Rita 'Oh, I expect they've been to a funeral.'

On returning to the farmhouse we said we had seen them. Frank had called at the farm several evenings previous to this. Floss told us that she and Frank had just got married. Within a couple of weeks her family had grown from two (her and her uncle) to five. Rita and I bought them a box of toffees for their wedding present. They seemed very pleased.

Frank was a very placid kind man and he spoke with a very broad country accent. He pronounced Biddenden as 'Bi-inen'. Floss pulled him up about that but he only laughed and so did she, in fact we found that Floss could really get the giggles, which she found hard to suppress. The tears would run down her face until she had found her piece of rag which she used as handkerchiefs. Uncle used to look so straight and disapproving, and none of us would dare look at one another.

Now we were going to school we were up early. Mr Bingham always had bread sop with warm milk which he slurped and I found that I had to concentrate very hard on my lovely bacon and eggs ('*One* egg – no, you have *two* as we have our own eggs'), so as not to giggle. I didn't want to be rude. Uncle always used a small pointed table knife which had worn down to a very sharp point over the years, to stab and pick up his food. Dinner and pudding were all eaten on the same dinner plate following a good clear-up of any tasty gravy, although Floss always gave me a fresh plate. We had lovely food, as there was a good supply of wild rabbits, chicken, milk, butter, vegetables and salad.

Soon Rita was rebilleted with her mother and I was on my own, but Floss and Mr Bingham were very kind and I loved being with Floss, collecting hen eggs from their nest all warm and feeling the soft feathers of the chicken as I gently raised them. One day Floss found a lot of dead chickens around the chicken huts and she told me that a fox had come and killed them, and that they killed just for the fun of it, not just one to eat and satisfy its hunger. I was very frightened because I thought the fox would come and get me and eat me all up, as I had read in my nursery rhyme books and stories. Floss comforted me and said I was mistaking a fox for a wolf, so I soon felt better.

I was ignorant about farm animals and wanted to know why bulls were kept when they didn't give any milk, but I can't remember getting any answer. I chased off a handsome cockerel who was having a fight with a hen, pecking her neck and jumping on her back. Floss

9

seemed amused at this, but I didn't know why. Soon I was given a small 'piggy porker' to bottle feed. He was the runt of the litter and would have to be hand-reared and I could help look after him. I was thrilled at this and he became very playful and would chase an old basket around his pen at great speed when he got older. He loved to converse, and snorted and grunted when spoken to, looking at me with intelligent eyes.

The men ate very heartily because of the strenuous work they performed. Frank started a further vegetable garden in a small paddock near the house which had a pond. One day I went with Floss to get some of the cucumbers which she grew on the top of a large manure compost heap and was so startled to see my normally composed guardian screaming and running like mad away from the heap. She quickly composed herself, not wanting to frighten me too, and just said, 'Snakes'!

Much later I was to experience my first sight of one when it slithered over my foot in deep undergrowth whilst out picking violets and primroses. I reacted the same as Floss, it was the unexpectedness of it. Thankfully it was very small, and it turned out that it was only a grass snake. In the summer when they shed their skins, I used the first one I ever found as a book mark for some of my class work. My teacher was not amused, but after all it was only the skin, and it was beautiful with its lace-like pattern.

Only a few days after Rita had left, another girl just 12, named Jean Driver, was billeted at the farm and it was good to have another companion. Within several weeks of our arrival both our parents came down to see our billet and were pleased to know we were being well looked after and had had a bath! Our lady social worker had called and organized the purchase of a large tin bath after one of us had mentioned at school that we hadn't had a bath for three weeks! This was taken in the kitchen and filled from the wood boiler in the kitchen with hot water. When we cleaned our teeth we pumped water from the pump at the end of the brick sink into a small hand bowl, and as it was pond water we grew adept in quickly plunging in the handle of the toothbrush into the centre of the bowl, and all the floating bits parted to allow a quick dip of the brush. Our parents worried that we might get typhoid, and a local doctor was approached on the matter, but he said he had no vaccine as all locals were bred and born there, and that we'd soon get used to it.

Within a few weeks we started to attend school full time as the village hall was made available for us, and this allowed the village children to resume their full-time education. I can picture our headmistress so well. Her name was Miss Muggfer and her grey hair was worn in plaits tightly coiled over each ear, looking like earphones. She was very, very stern. Miss Salvadori was my favourite teacher, she was beautiful with dark hair and brown eyes and seemed so gentle. She of course taught us Spanish.

Jean and I walked through the fields on the public footpaths to go to school. If we hurried it only took 25 minutes. The 2½ miles round the lanes took a lot longer. Floss packed us off with ample sandwiches all carefully wrapped in greaseproof paper, and a piece of cake for our lunch. On Sundays we had to attend church, and several of us were put in the choir whether we could sing or not. I certainly could not.

Soon Christmas was looming. Parents arranged for children to return home for the holiday. My father, who worked in London for a large newspaper firm, was able to afford a small car – which was a Morris Minor

11

or an Austin Seven, I'm not sure which – and he came to fetch me home. Our council house, which my parents had lived in since it was first built, looked so small, especially the narrow galley-type kitchen compared to the large farm one. I just stood and stared at each room. Floss had sent me home with some homemade butter and other goodies to help out our meagre rations. Farms were allowed a small quantity of anything they made, but all else had to be sold towards the war effort. When I went to bed the mattress felt strangely hard after the feather bed I had slept on at the farm.

It only took about another day to readjust. Thankfully I didn't see any signs of war about, in fact all seemed at peace. All too soon the time came for me to return to the farm. I didn't want to go back, and yet I did. These mixed-up feelings were so strange to me and my tummy started to twitch. I couldn't tell my parents either, because I didn't know what to say. Unfortunately my parents had not got on with each other for years, and I cannot hide the fact that it was not a happy home, and I hated the rows that went on at times. When I returned to the farm it looked so desolate, with only a large candle burning on the kitchen table. It wasn't long before Floss came along with a basin of eggs, having just fed and shut up the chickens for the night in their hen houses. Uncle was still out 'up The Buildings' as he had his own hens needing to be fed. Jean wasn't back yet and wasn't expected for a couple of days.

I said, 'I've tried to be brave but I can't be brave any longer,' and promptly burst into tears which was the first time I had done so.

I ate very little for two days and, as Floss was worried, she had the doctor, who examined me but found nothing amiss. I was pleased to see Jean return and soon bucked up no end, and somehow it encouraged me when I saw her going through the same emotions that I had felt on returning.

In later years I was to go through these types of feelings of not wanting to go home for holidays, and then when home, not wanting to go back, and yet so much wanting to be back. There was such a difference in my two homes. One with water, gas, electricity and a flush toilet and with trams running each way on our main road outside the house. The other a quiet farmhouse especially if I arrived back with no one around, with no fresh water, sanitation, gas or electricity.

In winter I had to walk the 2½ miles round the road from the village with my little suitcase all alone, as I had started to travel to and fro from Biddenden to Lewisham by coach where my Mum met me and then by tram to Downham Way where we lived and vice versa back to the farm.

On these journeys we were often stopped to be asked for identity cards or then, in my case, what was my reason for travelling, and I always carried a letter addressed to the farm from my parents which had my home address too. I remember one really long drawn-out journey on the coach when, for some reason, we were stopped a lot of times, and my mother gave up waiting at Lewisham for me. She thought I hadn't been able to come and that she had been late in meeting the coach and that it had gone. I caught the tram home and altogether it had been about a five-hour journey.

Frank, who had been courting Floss previous to my and Rita's arrival, came from a small village called Frittenden only a short distance from Biddenden, and worked on his father's land. He continued to do this, but gave Uncle and Floss a hand where and when

13

need. He was a kind, cheeky chappie, often teasing Floss until her eyes streamed with tears of laughter and out came her clean rag hanky to mop up and say 'Oh Frank!' He was what we would call now 'quite laid back', and Floss would have to remind him of things that needed to be done.

2

Winter started to set in with a vengeance, and as Jean and I walked across the fields to school the frost crackled and the odd blackbird, here and there, tossed up leaves from around the trunks of the trees, looking for insects. One day it was so cold the ponds iced over. Jean and I, who had been warned not to go on them because the ice might break, tested one with a firm foot tread. All seemed okay, and so we took a short-cut across instead of having to climb a stile and go round it. When we got home that afternoon from school, Floss was waiting for us, looking rather stern. She had been told that we had been seen crossing the icy pond beyond their land (there are many in Kentish fields). We were thoroughly told off for the danger we had placed ourselves in, plus the consequences if we had fallen through. Few people ever used those footpaths.

We wondered who had seen us but Floss wouldn't say, and we had to clean some brass as a reprimand. Out came brass and copper saucepans which had been arrayed on shelves and on top of a tall corner unit in the dining room plus candlesticks and other ornaments. It took us quite a time but we knew we had done wrong and what danger we had put ourselves in. We did tell the girls at school and elaborated a bit, saying 'We have been confined to barracks to clean the brass

15

for disobeying orders.' It sounded better and in keeping with the war efforts.

I remember seeing a little boy in a wheelchair, being pushed to school by his sister and accompanied by a teacher. I was dismayed, and thought he must have slipped on ice and broken something. No, his chilblains were so bad he couldn't walk. I had started to wear Wellingtons but as they wore out so quickly, with much use around the farm, I had to have the Dunlop boys' ones, which were much heavier. I felt for that little boy who must have suffered so much. I had cried, as I had seen Floss do with the 'Hot aches' in the warm kitchen, when our hands and feet began to warm up after being out in icy conditions. The weather grew colder and the kitchen became most inviting, with the stove throwing out considerable heat and crackling merrily when logs were added.

Delicious smells came from the oven as Floss baked all sorts of cakes, cheese and plain scones, meat and fruit pies. In the evening the sitting room would be warm, the fire having been lit in the late afternoon. Bramley apples would be eaten which Floss previously had collected from under Uncle's four-poster bed where they had been laid out to store. Uncle and Frank then enjoyed their small glass of cider, poured from a seemingly small jug, but this was Uncle's special cider which had been left to mature for several years. Floss would chat to Jean and I, or we did some mending or darning. Otherwise the silence was only broken by Uncle's well-aimed spit into the logs on the fire, which sizzled and sent sparks making a maze of different colours for a few seconds as they intertwined through the flames. He was very clever with his aim from his carver chair, set beside the fireplace and just in front of the chaise longue type sofa where Jill the dog was snoozing. Jean and I were off to bed at about 8.30 p.m., followed by the others at about 9.30 p.m. The chimney-breasts ran up through the house, keeping the brickwork warm, and we were all soon rested down into our cosy feather beds which tucked all around us as our bodies sank into the middle.

Winter settled in with a vengeance and the first snow fell. It was so beautiful seeing the fresh sparkling white of the untrodden snow, and the trees hidden under their heavy top knots. Jean and I went through the fields to school and it was like wonderland. One morning, when we awoke to a bright day, we couldn't believe our eyes. The lanes were full of enormous snow drifts 6 feet high, leaning and covering hedges, making large swirls resembling ice cream blocking up everything. Jean and I decided we must try to go to school. We were so eager to get out and explore the fields. Floss was too worried with the problems of cattle feeding and getting to her hens, and Frank and Uncle too had animals to tend. Jean and I set off but, having made our way so slowly across half the first field we had to admit defeat as the snow fell into the tops of our Wellingtons. We were frozen to the marrow by the time we reached the farm. The chilblains then started but were never so bad as that little boy's. We were unable to go to school for nearly three weeks – there was no way through.

Frank had bought a wireless, which we all thought wonderful. It was only used in the evenings, as farm life takes up so much time. Even in the winter, ditching, fencing and general repairs have to be done, and the stock cleaned out and fed. I developed a nasty painful sty on my eye and when it eventually cleared up, I went on to have two more. There was no treatment, and one's immune system had to fight the infection. It

17

was the same with colds or a headache – aspirin was never used at the farm.

By this time we evacuees and our teachers had taken over the village hall for our lessons, enabling the village children and ourselves to continue our full-time education. The mayor and mayoress from Lewisham came to visit us one day, and I have a couple of photos of that event. We all had to take a packed lunch to school and I loved the way Floss wrapped our sandwiches with greaseproof paper before putting them in a tin box plus some cake or a scone and apple.

Winter turned to spring and I went out with Mr Bingham to go 'lookerin', which meant counting his sheep. He took a bag of corn and once in the sheep field he called out 'Cor barr, cor barr'. The sheep lifted their heads from grazing and soon came running. One or two were very brave, pushing in front of others trying to be first and trying to put their heads in the sack. Mr Bingham explained that they had been bottle reared and so had no fear of humans. I started to notice that each sheep had different facial characteristics and Mr Bingham called some by name.

Soon lambing started and I was so thrilled when I was given one of a pair of twins to carry to a pen. They had to have shelter as they were very tiny. Mother followed after us as the lambs were bleating loudly despite their small size. I shall always remember the lamb's dampish creamy, yellow and slightly harsh, tight curly coat.

Soon Floss had some 'sock' lambs in the kitchen near the stove which had to be bottle-fed day and night for a time. I was so pleased when I could help feed one or other of these lambs, holding them under their chins where milk dribbled out of the sides of their mouths as they greedily sucked and pulled at the teat. The bottle had to be well tilted up so that the lamb didn't suck air and blow up its stomach.

I went out rabbiting with Mr Bingham and Frank, but was told very firmly that I must always keep behind them, which I did as they each had a gun. Jill the spaniel used to go mad with excitement when she saw them, but even she knew the rules and followed all the commands what and what not to do. In a way I hated seeing rabbits shot, but there were a lot of them and Floss would skin them and, after gutting them, make a wonderful casserole with onion and freshly chopped sage. The skins were stretched on a board and treated, as were mole skins, and then sold when dried out.

Mr Bingham had a yellow ferret with pink-red eyes, which was kept in a small cage with lots of hay. I was told I must never touch him as he could bite straight through my finger. He was used for flushing rabbits out from their burrows. Nets were set up over the burrow holes to catch the poor rabbits and then they were held head downwards by their back legs, and quickly and expertly thumped on the back of their heads. I used to help, by listening with my ear to the ground on one of the sections of burrow for the thumping of the rabbit's feet as he raced along towards an exit away from the ferret. Sometimes a ferret would 'lay up' and kill the rabbit in the burrow and then start to make a meal of it. The meant a lot of trouble and work, and the burrows had to be dug out to try and find it. It was a real problem which took ages, as the ferret had to be caught. I had begun to learn the two sides of farming – birth and death of animals – the latter was a harsh reality which I always found hard to accept.

Later I was to have a pet rabbit of my own, which I

had always yearned for – a rabbit I could look after and love, a rabbit which didn't have to be shot, netted or eaten by a ferret. This came about when an uncle and aunt of mine were bombed out from their London home. My uncle kept a number of rabbits, and the surviving ones had to be found homes. Floss agreed I could have one, and my mother brought him down by coach. He was very much a mongrel having the same looks and colour of a wild rabbit except for a large V-shaped patch of snowy white fur between his eyes and I was told he was a buck rabbit.

I adored him, and soon learned about the wild plants on which to feed him, which I gathered with great interest from fields and verges. Mr Bingham gave me a small swede which I paid him 2d for. It made me feel most responsible for my young charge. Frank built the hutch and Floss provided corn and meal. I called him Beauty, his fur was so thick with a lustrous shine.

I didn't like to think of him being kept in a cage all the time so once a day I used to let him out for a run in the Barn Field. He used to keep quite close to heel, then dart forward, half turning on his front paws, whilst his hind legs gave a joyous kick high into the air. Sometimes he would lag behind and devour a dandelion, watching I didn't get too far ahead, then would come rushing past me, ending up with a delightful kick in the air. I'm afraid I spoilt Beauty with his runs, because he began to dislike the captivity of his cage and was forever gnawing holes in his hutch which had to be patched up. He was very affectionate and would lick my face and neck when I carried him.

One morning, when I went to feed him, I was welcomed by an empty hutch. He had escaped through the hole he had gnawed in the wire netting in the front of the cage. I began a frenzied search for him in the garden and the Barn Field. Just as I was about to give up, Beauty came popping innocently out of the hedge. This adventure was repeated several times.

Several weeks later, when I went to feed him, I found a pile of fur enclosing a nest of nine babies in a corner at the back of the hutch. Beauty was a 'she' and not a 'he', and must have mated with a wild rabbit. There was much amusement when I went rushing back to tell Floss, Frank and Mr Bingham.

After most of her litter had been parted from her, she still persisted in her escapades. I couldn't bear to keep her caged any longer, but decided to let her have her freedom. Floss thought it was for the best too, and let her go free in a nearby field close to a chicken house. Next morning I went with Floss to open up the chicken house and feed the hens. Who should come running, or rather hopping along, to meet us but Beauty and she ate the wet meal along with the chickens. After that she was there both morning and evenings.

I placed an old chicken coop, filled with hay, behind the hen house, in which she could sleep. She lived this glorious life of freedom and liberty for just three months until a fox killed her, having previously killed 25 hens. We found her remains in a little field left of the hen house. The fox had made a meal of her, except for her head which was lying in the grass with the white V on her forehead. Floss was as upset as I was.

Most of the evacuees were well spread out in Biddenden but, a girl named Betty Blackmore lived half a mile down the lane and used to cycle up on an old bike which I think belonged to her billet. She let me have turns on it, and in no time I had mastered how to ride. When I wrote home the news that I could do this, my father said that he would get me a bike, as he was well aware of the long distance I had to walk when going via the road to school. I was so surprised and happy at this news, and it wasn't long before I received the letter that the bike was being sent to Biddenden railway station. On telling my teacher about this she allowed me, and another girl to accompany me, to hurry down from the village hall to the station to see if it had arrived. This was to be during our lunchtime break, of course we had to be back in time for lessons. I was so excited and so was my friend as we hurried off. I remember a large hut at the station but it was shut and no one was about. We managed to stand on some low railings to enable us to look through the windows, and were disappointed to see not a single bike.

The teacher advised that we were to wait another week before we went again. What a long week that seemed. However, the day came when we were allowed with ever-growing excitement to go again. This time we both climbed onto the railings to peer through the windows, without bothering to look for anyone in uniform. *Yes*, there were two bikes! One looked very big and rather old-fashioned and was brown, probably with rust. The other certainly wasn't mine as it had drop curvy handlebars and rat trap shiny pedals. The frame was pale blue as far as I could make out between its wrappings.

The station master appeared and said, 'Are you the young ladies looking for the arrival of a bike?' I said I was, but it hadn't arrived yet, and sighed my great disappointment.

'Is your name Georgina Plumb?' he asked.

I said, 'Yes.'

'Well it has arrived – it's that one,' he said, pointing to the sports bike.

I just couldn't believe my eyes. Soon it was unwrapped and after a few attempts I was safe enough to ride it back to school with my friend running beside me with a promise she could have a go later on.

Mr Bingham, Floss and Frank were also pleased to see the lovely bike and provided me with rags to clean and polish it so that I could keep it in its prime state. Not long after, Jean's parents provided her with one. We kept them in the corn lodge on the right-hand side of the privy. I really was so grateful to my father and wrote to tell him. I later learned that the bike had been made up from various bits of bikes, hence it did not carry any brand name. This didn't bother me as it felt special being made for me.

Some of the evacuees changed billets for one reason or other. I was so lucky to be with Floss, Frank and Mr Bingham. More children were beginning to go home, as their parents thought it safe enough as things were quiet on the war front. Although Jean hadn't settled into farm life as well as I had, she was happy enough if she could look at the newspaper. Jean also knew a bit about ballroom dancing, and she taught me some basic steps of the waltz and quick step. One day Floss felt tempted to have a go too. She tried the radio and found some suitable music. Then looking through the sitting room window past Uncle's beehives and the front field, liberally dotted with tufts of rushes up to the buildings, she checked that she could see Uncle working up there. Then hastily she urged us to help her move the large table and chairs to the side of the room, and we started to try out our dancing steps with her. It was a magical moment and we laughed and laughed as we fell over each others' feet with Floss turning into a girl playing truant and enjoying herself away from the constant round of work.

But all too soon, and still with her eye on the toing and froing of Uncle, she said 'Quick, we must put the furniture back, Uncle will soon be back. Don't tell him we have been dancing.'

On a rare occasion Floss and Frank, who almost never got out for a break, decided to walk to the village and go to the Red Lion, and they said they would take Jean and I as a treat and we could have a soft drink. It seemed very cosy and jolly at the pub, and Jean and I just sat enjoying the experience, watching the grown-ups enjoying themselves. Most of all I enjoyed the walk home, along the road which was well lit by a full moon and twinkling stars, as large trees made spooky shapes. It was a one-off treat not to be repeated, as Frank was later enlisted in the Home Guard, underwent training, and had to be on duty in the evenings.

I began to get friendly with a village girl who was the same age as myself and who had been born in the small cottage opposite East Ongley farmhouse. She had an Auntie Joyce and an Uncle George, and a grandmother, who lived in a pair of cottages near to the small path leading through the fields to the village. My friend's name was Dorothy Watts. We were both about the same height and of skinny build, but our backgrounds were so different, with me coming from London, that we took time to get to know each other. She was very attuned to nature, as I was becoming, and I was eager to learn more as we walked the lanes together picking all sorts of wild flowers of which she knew the names. Often I was collecting leaves for my pet rabbit Beauty, and she would help me. Dorothy told me she had an elder brother named Alec and a younger brother called Peter, and I told her of my brother Ivon who had by then returned home from his billet at Newbury, and as soon as he was old enough had enlisted in the RAF.

I got to know her Mum and Dad and I loved the cosy atmosphere of the small cottage in which she lived. They too had no electricity, gas or mains water, but this was the norm for most of the outlying village homes. There was a warmth to the gentle glow of candles and oil lamps, and the fire's glow from the hearths and cooking stoves.

On the corner bend where East Ongley farmhouse stood was the entrance to Ibornden Park which had two pillars and a waist-high wall each side. There was a private drive through acres of fields with several ponds and large trees up to a mansion which was barely visible from the road except for the very tall tops of the chimneys. Soon there was lots of activity with army platoons taking over the mansion for billeting and training and whatever. Soldiers stood in sentry boxes placed by each pillar of the entrance. From being a quiet lane, there was much activity for a while, but then it became peaceful again. One day a handsome sergeant, though he did look stern, called at the farm house for a dozen fresh eggs if Floss had any for sale. He came a few more times and we made Floss laugh when Jean and I dashed to where he had stood in the kitchen when he had gone. We were very young, 12 years old then. Ibornden was supposed to be haunted by the ghost of a young girl in the park near to where she was drowned. No other soldiers came to the house except for a young private who had a small motorbike and asked if he could house it in the lodge leading to the privy, as he wasn't supposed to have the machine. Mr Bingham had to be consulted and he wasn't too happy, but said 'Yes'. It wasn't there very long and soon both bike and soldier were no longer seen. Jean and I were warned not to go over and speak to the sentries on guard, and we didn't.

One morning when we awoke, Floss told us to peep out of the window, and we heard Mr Bingham and Frank talking in hushed tones from the other bedrooms. Everywhere in the garden, along the hedges, against every wall and tree, were lines of sleeping exhausted-looking infantry soldiers, some with boots and socks off, if not most of them. They were passing through en route for somewhere and had come so silently to rest, no one had heard them. I shall always remember that sight, but I remember nothing of their leaving – perhaps Jean and I had gone to school. Floss said that they had to tell the soldiers which pond was the source from where the pump in the farm kitchen drew its pond water. Floss wasn't so keen on the thought of all those poor sweaty feet in it!

Jean still wasn't adapting so well to being an evacuee, and her parents took her home. She was never replaced by anyone else. I did miss her for a time, and Floss suggested I may like to move into the small bedroom at the back of the house. I took to this room very much and it didn't feel so lonely.

I was enjoying farm life more and more, as Floss taught me to fish in the farm ponds. She cut a couple of long straight branches from a tree and tied on some old fishing line she had found. A cork was added for a float and the end quill of a feather pushed down into it. With the line and an old hook, this made perfect fishing tackle. Floss stayed with me for as long as she could, and enjoyed catching the odd stickleback then tossing them back into the water just as much as I did. Later when I knew all the safest places to stand around the ponds, Floss allowed me to go off on my own. If she could find an odd 20 minutes from all her chores she would come to see how I was doing.

I never felt lonely – so much to see, hear and smell, such as the water mint which grew around the edge of the pond, and the rustling amongst the bulrushes with their lovely brown furry looking heads. These I was warned not to pick and take indoors as when broken they made a terrible mess with seeded fluff everywhere. Then there were birds and the occasional duck, or mice, rats and rabbits. I would describe the birds and Floss told me their names. My senses became even more acute and I could spot birds' nests very quickly, but I would never steal an egg. I found a snake skin and added that to my collection of book marks.

I used to like helping Floss, and everything I did was because I wanted to and not because it was expected of me. I always found the cream separator a laborious job to dry with its many, many discs, which Floss had to wash every day. All cloths were boiled and turned out snowy white despite the pond water, which incidentally had to be brought in by buckets from a further but larger pond, when drought lowered the nearer one to sludge and muck. After a week or more of cream collecting it was put into the wooden butter churn and was rhythmically turned by a side handle at a constant medium pace until it turned to butter. This took some considerable time, and some days it would take longer than others. It could be very tiring to the arm and frustrating for Floss with stock feeding to do plus her family to feed, mending animal pens and egg washing and so on. I felt so pleased when Floss let me take a turn to churn the butter, as it was a serious job and I took the handle in unison as she let go so as not to disturb the rhythm.

Although Floss may be in the kitchen and I was in

the dairy room along the passage, if I did get the urge to turn the handle just a little bit faster, Floss would call, 'Butter won't come any faster if you do that.'

What a joy it was to hear the sudden splash and plonk when suddenly it turned to butter. Then I could watch the master (Floss) at work as she slapped and shaped the butter into oblong blocks with wooden butter pats which sent the buttermilk spattering out in all directions. Then with a last expert slap on the top to make a line pattern, the butter was ready to be stored in the cool pantry. In the summer the last blocks of butter did tend to go rank, but we did have to finish them up. Apart from that, it was the most lovely butter I had ever tasted. Nothing, even to this day, has come up to that taste.

I was fascinated by the deft way Frank sawed and split the large logs, putting them into neat piles in the lodge, ready for the stove or fireplaces. Frank put aside some of the smaller logs for me to split, as I was itching to have a go. He gave me a small axe and laughed when it got stuck in the middle of a log and I could do nothing with it, but gradually I got the knack. I knew the dangers, and was always very careful how I set the log on the large chopping block, with my legs well out of the way, and aiming down with the axe. I often went out into The Lodge and split up a nice pile of small logs and found it pleasing to do.

Egg washing I had a go at too, as they had to be wiped all over before being packed; then a man came to collect them to sell. I didn't do this very often as Mr Bingham did the majority, sitting by the glow of candle-light and warmth of the kitchen stove. It was a job he enjoyed. Just now and then, not very often, an egg would drop on to the brick kitchen floor with a resounding crack as he let go of it, momentarily falling

Gina aged 11 years at East Ongley Farm, Biddenden, Kent in September 1939.

Gina and one of the calves at East Ongley Farm, Biddenden, Kent 1939.

Gina gives Piggy Porky a drink, 1939.

Biddenden, Kent 1939, Village Hall, Downham Central School, evacuees from Bromley, Kent with Mayor and Mayoress of Lewisham SE6. Gina above white spikes of open gate wearing large white collared blouse.

Gilletts, Smarden, Kent, June 1943

6th year at Gilletts, July 1943. Gina under chin of tallest girl back row left.

Gina helping on the farm feeding calves

Gina with a bottle reared lamb

Frank Wheadon

Gina with her best friend Boxer

Boxer, Gina and Frank

Gina with Daisy

Floss Wheadon with Daisy

Floss Wheadon - Gina's guardian

Walter Bingham in the oast house,
East Ongley Farm, Biddenden, Kent
pressing dried hops.

Walter Bingham - Floss's
uncle at East Ongley Farm
with Jill.

asleep. Sometimes he had been up and out in the night, if he had heard a cow bellowing, to see if all was well. He hated high winds or the dog barking in the night, when again he would get up, taking his gun with him. I thought he was very brave, and snuggled further down into my warm feather bed, feeling safe and sound, if I heard him go.

Boxer, a semi-retired, pale dappled grey Shire horse, who had been given to Mr Bingham to help with light work, was the love of my life. I had always loved horses and felt an affinity with them. One day Mr Bingham was 'hop shimming' with an implement to dig and loosen the soil in-between the rows of hops. Boxer pulled this whilst Mr Bingham guided the implement from two handles. I helped by walking at Boxer's head. He seemed to fall asleep one day, stopping, and wouldn't budge. Mr Bingham went to the hedge and broke off a small stick.

As he came towards Boxer I clearly remember saying, 'You hit me before you hit that horse.'

Mr Bingham looked both startled and amused, and I felt all mixed up as I had been taught never to be rude, but Boxer was my friend. However he hastily obliged when I said a loud 'Gee up, Boxer,' and off we went again, all forgiven and forgotten.

One day some official-looking men came from the Government to see Mr Bingham. I was later to understand that the farmland was not being used to its full potential, and it would now have to produce more crops towards the war effort of feeding the nation. East Ongley Farm must have a tractor to do this work, and Frank would take on this extra labour and assist Mr Bingham. Frank was able to drive tractors. Floss would have more hens, and help rear more calves. More hops were to be grown too. Of course I did not know all the ins and outs of this arrangement, but life got busier and busier on the farm. Floss cared very much for her animals and would never send any of her cattle to market, or to be slaughtered, without getting up very early to give them a good feed.

Boxer continued to do light work, helping to bring in hay from the fields to the barn, but he was an old horse and one day wasn't well. I went off to school knowing that a vet was coming to see him. I was heartbroken to hear, on my return, that he had had to be put down. It was done quickly with a humane killer, and I cannot bring myself to describe this though I was told, but had never seen one.

About six months later I was told to go up The Buildings and look in one of the milking sheds. I was a bit wary because coming home from school, on my bike, and passing The Buildings out would come the big old gander at great speed with his huge wings splayed out, hissing like mad and trying to attack my foot on the pedal nearest to him. When he had young- sters about he could be very aggressive. I thought I'd better carry a bucket with me as it had saved me one time when he had silently crept up behind me with wings outstretched and I had to swing it around me to protect myself.

Anyway I had the most wonderful surprise when I did look into the shed, for there stood another beauti- ful dappled grey Shire horse, looking very much like Boxer except his colouring was so much darker. I later learned that they get paler in colour as they get older. I hurried back to the house to ask if he was staying, and when they said 'Yes,' I was over the moon. When I asked his name they said Boxer, of course. Any horse of theirs was a Boxer.

We soon became friends too and I was allowed to

bring him up from the fields into his stable for Mr Bingham or Frank to feed him and bed him down. One day I was leading him and we had to go through a five-barred gate. It was a bit old and rickety, and I had to lift it clear to lead him through. Usually he was patient and stood waiting. Not so this day. He pushed it with his chest and it came away from its hinges and fell flat to the ground, and he stomped clean over it.

I managed to catch up with him and said, 'How am I going to tell them what you have done! I don't know if I'll be allowed to get you any more.' I was really worried.

I needn't have been. They said they had needed a new gate there for ages, and Boxer was just trying to help!

Sometimes Frank would make a step with his hands for me to tread in so that I could get onto Boxer's back, which was so wide. He really was a big horse. If Frank was in one of his mischievous moods he would get the horse trotting with me hanging onto his mane for dear life.

3

A dramatic change was to start in my school life, as so many children had returned home. A good many had reached the working age of 16 over the past couple of years. Others had returned for all manner of reasons. Our few teachers were now needed back at Downham Central in Bromley. We remaining children were to join up with the Catford Central School whose billets were in both Smarden and Bethersden. Smarden was about 5 miles from Biddenden and Bethersden was about 4 miles the other side of Smarden. It had been arranged that we were to be picked up by car at the top of Biddenden High Street. I was to cycle to the village and leave my bike in a garage to the side of a house close by. The thing I remember most was this very big posh car stopping and a small thin man, dressed in a suit, got out to speak to Miss Salvadori who was our only teacher left. She was to stay with us for a while, travelling with us and helping to teach at Smarden Catford Central. The car was a Canadian Buick which had been brought into use to ferry the schoolgirls billeted in Bethersden to the house called Gilletts used now as their school, in Smarden. Mr Small was the owner of this most beautiful very large car and he now had to ferry us to school, and another man named Mr Weeks was to take over his previous 'run' of the Bethersden girls. The car ran so smoothly you could have drunk a cup of tea without spilling a drop. Mr Small was a man of few words, and we were equally quiet once in the car. It all seemed a dream.

It wasn't long (perhaps all too quickly as if it was magical) we arrived into the drive of Gilletts, a most imposingly big house surrounded with large grounds. Mrs Blundell met us, she was the headmistress, short and of nicely rounded motherly proportions, with greying hair and rather heavy lines on her top lip. We followed her with great wonder and awe as she showed us around the many rooms and corridors of the house.

'Always come down this staircase,' she said, which we could see was the main stairway because of its size. 'I will show you the smaller back staircase, which you will always use to go up. You must never run.'

Her voice was kind, and as we saw there were so many pupils and so many bedrooms being used as classrooms, this made sense without needing further comment. There was a huge kitchen with two ladies busy preparing delicious smelling meals.

'The kitchen is strictly out of bounds, girls,' she said with emphasis, as our mouths watered. The main room, with French windows suitably away from the kitchen smells, resembled the size of a really large hall and was used for assembly, gym, school plays, lunch times for all pupil's dinners and 'play time' when weather was too bad to go outside. One of the small rooms upstairs was used by a visiting dentist, doctor or nurses, or a Mrs Derby who was matron-cum-mother. The Catford girls were the ones to tell us about this and all seemed to refer to it as The Dentist's room, with some trepidation in their voices. Up to then I had always cycled the 7 miles to Tenterden with other girls who could do so from Biddenden and back, for check-up and

33

treatment. I was used to cycling with Floss on rare occasions when she was able to get out to visit sisters in that area, the journey by bike didn't bother me.

The Downham girls were then split up, taken into various classrooms according to age and ability. My teacher was to be Miss Chaplin. A very tall pleasant girl whose name was Brenda Southgate, and her friend Janet, took me under their wing and I soon began to take this new situation in my stride. Janet was the quieter of my two new friends, but they both had happy, bubbly natures and a sense of humour which I enjoyed. They were very clever too and were a part of a team of girls picked out to study for their Oxford School Certificate, but all this was a year or two later.

Mrs Derby informed me that I could go on the weekly bath rota which was for any children billeted in homes without a bathroom and hot water. Each class had a rota with their permitted time slots. Pupils were allowed 15 minutes each to be absent from class for their bath and the bath must be cleaned after each person. The timing was strict but sometimes we swapped around if it was during a subject we didn't care for. It was done with minimum fuss as we quietly left the room and returned rosy and clean.

The grounds had many very large, beautiful trees, and there was a huge walnut tree outside the back kitchen. A lot of the ground had been taken over to grow vegetables and fruit which was used in the kitchen to feed the large number of children, which included the village schoolchildren. They were only a short distance up the road and joined us for their midday meal. The older girls helped with the very young children from the village and also were on a roster for serving duties.

All pupils at Gilletts had to spend a short time each

week helping the gardener to weed, hoe, pick up stones, sew seeds, collect vegetables and so on. Mr Wilmshurst was the gardener of Gilletts before it was used as a school for evacuees. He was a kind, patient man, but woe betide anyone who didn't brush clean and then wipe the implements they had used with one of the many slightly oiled rags, before hanging them up on the neat rows of hooks in the shed. It was a good habit to learn, and one I have used all my life.

Things were beginning to hot up on the war front and still more Downham Central children returned home as they reached the age of 16. On returning home for one of the school holidays I found our lounge dominated by a huge Morrison table shelter, with cage-like guards all around the base.

We began to hear the air raid sirens in Biddenden. Enemy planes droned in the night skies as they headed for London or other targets on which to drop their bombs. Floss, Frank and I used to stand in the passage between kitchen running down to the pantry room. Mr Bingham hurriedly joined us, having stopped to collect the strong metal hand basin with wooden handle and placed on his head. Floss looked at me, and I felt a sudden fit of the giggles rising up inside me. Floss's eyes were beginning to water with suppressed laughter and we daren't look at Frank, knowing he also would see the comical side of the first of many frightening situations. Poor Uncle really did tremble with fright, which was sad to see.

It was decided to bring our beds down into the dining room, making it very cramped, and none of us slept very well. I could hear the mice scuttling in the outside cavity walls close to my head, no doubt missing the warmth of the log fire which couldn't now be lit. This situation didn't last long thankfully, as the farm was issued with an Anderson shelter which was soon dug into position not far from the kitchen door. We all returned to our bedrooms and a good night's sleep.

We were to see more army convoys passing the farm house on their way to Ibornden Park House. Others had left silently in the night. Again on odd occasions a single soldier would call at the farmhouse asking to buy some eggs, probably to take home on leave. Guards were still on sentry duty close by, but they must have turned a blind eye, as I think the farm was still out of bounds. Communication was very limited those days. And for strangers there was a lack of signposts and mileage information.

Bombs were being dropped around us as some of the German bombers decided to jettison their load once over the Channel and hot-foot it home. London was too risky for them. Some high-explosive bombs were dropped in Smarden, three in Gillett's front garden and two in the paddock. The clay was soft with the very wet weather, so they caused very little damage. Thankfully we weren't there when it happened.

I was enjoying the extra curriculum that Catford Central could provide in the spacious house and grounds of Gilletts and the rides to and fro from Biddenden in the Buick. As Mr Small got to know us better, he became more conversational. My favourite teacher, who was the only Downham Central teacher we had, was called back to London too. The few that were left at Biddenden were now on their own in the village, but we all had good billets. One girl didn't turn up for school for three weeks and Mrs Blundell asked if I would cycle out to her billet at Three Chimneys, some 2½ plus miles further out from the village than I was, but in that direction. I think she was thoroughly run down and poorly.

With the loss of Miss Salvadori our Spanish lessons were dropped and we started to learn French like all the other pupils. The gym in the big hall was great, with plenty of room to try the vaulting horse. Some of the girls were very good at it and thundered up and over it. There were games of rounders too in the paddock and wasn't I pleased when I heard the lovely 'crack' as I swung the baton for the umpteenth time and actually hit the ball.

'Don't throw your baton down, you will hit someone, just drop it!' said the teacher in charge at the time.

On some of the very hot summer days we enjoyed our dinner out in the garden under the trees. It was like a big happy family, with Mrs Blundell being such a kind caring head of staff which was also reflected in her teachers.

We children did have our worries as we heard of the terrible air raids back home. My brother was training for the air crew and my father had been called up and went into the RAF as well, as a mechanical engineer.

Another good fun activity we were allowed to do in the main hall when the weather was bad, following our dinner, was ballroom dancing. Once the hall was cleared of chairs and tables, out came an old gramophone and some old records and girls paired up ready to practice. There would be much stumbling and tripping with many of us, who were definitely learners, especially when taking the man's forward steps position. Older girls who were more used to the steps would change partners and steer us around with many 'ohs' and 'ouches', and 'Mind where you're going' comments.

I continued to enjoy Dorothy's company as we searched for flowers and wild grasses. A particular one was called 'toddling grass' and she pointed it out to me and how the pretty rounded shaped seed heads, like small rounded feet, gently 'toddled' in the breeze. After it had been well dried by the sun on the plant, we picked just a few pieces and they lasted ages and didn't drop. In some counties I have since learned it is called 'quaking grass' and has all but disappeared.

Alec, Dorothy's older brother, came up to work on West Ongley Farm and lodged with his grandmother in the cottage nearby. He made me think of my own brother who I greatly missed and only saw if he was home on leave when my school holiday coincided with it. Alec was a great teaser, as was my brother when I was young. He tied a dead grass snake around a gatepost I had to go through after finding out I wasn't at all keen on them. Another time when cycling down Beach Lane I saw an old tin in the middle of the road and cycled past it. Then curiosity got the better of me and I turned back and opened it, to find a snake's skin! Well, that didn't frighten me. Alec said he knew I would be curious and look.

Gilletts had started a branch of the Young Farmers' Club and I was glad to become a member, joining in the rabbit section. We couldn't get attached to them as they were reared to be slaughtered by the local butcher and used as food. There was a poultry section, a guinea pig section, also bee and a gardening section. All this helped towards our war effort as produce was sold. We certainly led busy lives and I cannot ever remember any squabbling though there may have been. Our responsibilities were taken seriously and required self-discipline not only in our school work, but in our billets as well. One day an army officer asked Mrs Blundell if her girls could possibly help out with some darning of socks for his platoon. She readily agreed and the older girls were presented with a huge pile of army socks and wool and large needles with which to repair them. One of the teachers gave a brief lesson on the correct way to darn, making sure to push the needle up then down across each thread previously laid in lines across the hole until it had been neatly filled. This mission was done very caringly and lovingly by the girls. I poked a tiny piece of paper down into one of the pairs I mended, with the words 'May your toes never grow cold.' I wonder if the soldier got it. Mrs Blundell said she had examined all the darns and praised us for our very good work. Later she read out a letter of appreciation from the officer and his men.

Another job we did whenever we could find time was to collect rosehips from the hedges. We took them to school where they were weighed. When a sufficient amount had been collected they were sent away to be made into rosehip syrup which was a rich source of vitamin C.

I had started to go home by train, first travelling from Biddenden to Maidstone by bus, then catching a train to Bromley South Station, where my mother usually met me and another bus to the bottom of Downham Way. I remember that first journey vividly. My mother had written saying that when I was on the platform I was to look out for a nice lady and to get into a compartment, with her for the journey. There were very few people about but there was a very nice lady nearby and I followed her. We were the only two people in the compartment but neither of us spoke. I was used to travelling on my own, though not on trains. Along came an inspector asking to see our tickets.

On inspecting mine he said, 'That will be something shillings and pence please' (I can't remember the sum).

I opened my purse and managed to find enough, but

with only a few pence left. I didn't understand why I had to give him this money but I couldn't bring myself to ask. I was worried if my mother didn't meet me at Bromley I would not have enough for my bus fare from Bromley to home. Thank goodness, she was there, and on telling her my story she asked if the carriage had arm rests and I said it did.

'You were in a first-class carriage,' she said. How unworldly and young I was. Another lesson learned.

Air raids were getting worse and we started to use the Anderson shelter when hearing the familiar drone of the German bombers going overhead in our region. We all hated being in that cramped cold shelter and wouldn't use it, preferring to stand in a deep ditch just behind the back of the farmhouse. At least we wouldn't be buried under a pile of bricks. At times I took a lot of persuasion to get out of my snug feather bed and awaken myself from the sleep I badly needed. In the morning when the postman arrived he brought news of a German bomber which had been shot down, and of a farmer finding one of the crew sitting on his doorstep to surrender himself. The Battle of Britain, as we now knew it, was being fought overhead too and I remember a day-time raid when small planes – Spitfires – were chasing all over the shop, then out of the sky came several parachutes. One figure appeared to be swinging round and round. One of the farm-hands from West Ongley said 'That's a dead 'un.' I only hoped he was a German. We didn't know who any of them were really, but that picture stays well in my mind.

One Easter I went home on holiday from school. I was to experience one of the worst raids on London, or perhaps I should say the run-up to it. I was terrified by the heavy barrage fire from our ack-ack guns. It was a constant barrage as they fought to bring the enemy planes down. My mother sent me back to the farm next day.

A few Christmas holidays, I didn't get home for one reason or another. With rationing I was only able to buy a few sweets and so managed to save quite a few pence from my pocket money and felt so pleased to be able to buy my mother a very pretty pink lacy patterned bed-jacket from a ladies' shop at the end of the high street in Biddenden. Another time, when goods were getting very short in London, I sent a small Christmas parcel of kitchen items, such as tea cloths, pot scourers and a bar of soap. Mother was especially pleased with the pot scourers. On the farm, Christmas was the same as any other day, stock to be fed, milking to be done and so on. I cannot remember seeing any Christmas cards or presents exchanged. It seemed perfectly natural to me and everyone else, and I didn't question it.

I did love to go up to the milking stable in the winter with its warmth from the cows, the soft glow from a lamp, hearing the steady swoosh noise as milk was stripped from the cows' teats into the galvanized buckets.

Mr Bingham would take his small milking stool onto the next cow and say, 'Set foot, set foot,' and the cow would step back with her back foot to allow him to milk her.

If Frank was helping to milk he would turn his cap round so he could lean his head against the cow and would direct the first milk into any cat's open mouth – they were expert at catching it.

One day Floss came hurrying back from a field asking me to come quickly, as Frank and she needed help in getting a cow that was calving and in a difficult

41

labour, back up to The Buildings. I was to coax the heavy-laden cow with a hand bowl of her favourite food, whilst Floss walked at her head and Frank gave gentle persuasion from the rear. It was the first time I had ever seen a cow calving, and there were two small legs with dainty hooves sticking out from her bottom. We did get her up and into the stable but it was a slow process and at times she bellowed loudly. I wasn't allowed to stay, and nothing was explained to me.

Once when going for a ride on my bike I noticed a cow in the yard of West Ongley Farm with what I thought was all its stomach coming out of its bottom in a red mass reaching to the ground. I hurriedly turned my bike round and raced back to tell Floss, and she calmly told me it was the cow's afterbirth and that she was all right. I was learning as situations presented themselves. They were never talked over.

I hated to see animals suffering and so did Floss. One of her pet lambs, which she had reared on the bottle, had twin lambs, but the births had caused her to be paralysed in her hindquarters. Floss had her brought down to the farmhouse and laid her on a patch of grass near to the kitchen door. There wasn't much hope for her but she happily grazed lying down and I would go and lift her by her hindquarters while she hobbled on two front legs and seemed glad to do so. We knew this couldn't go on so, after a couple of days, she was put down. We were both sad.

Joy soon follows on the heels of those sad moments, such as when a calf is born, though I never did witness a complete birth. Floss would say, 'Come and look,' soon after if I was about. The calves were so beautiful after their mother had licked them clean. Their coats shone and were rich in colour. The large eyes with their long eyelashes would be the envy of any girl. The

42

large wet nose with wide sniffing nostrils would point up to my face blowing gentle puffs of sweet breath over me whilst the calf sways on over-long wobbly legs and the mother lows proudly, watching close by.

Great fun would come later when a calf was weaned from its mother. I watched Floss, who had the patience of a saint, holding a bucket of warm gruel in-between her knees to begin with, trying to entice the calf to suck by putting her fingers in the calf's mouth, drawing its nose down, whilst pushing on its head, hopefully into the bucket. The calf would either respond by hastily withdrawing its head from the warm gruel and blowing it out from wet nostrils all over the person holding the bucket, or it would buck and thrash its head with amazing strength and the entire contents would go flying all over the bucket holder. By then the calf wasn't trusting anybody. More gruel had to be made and, if I was nearby to give a hand, I would. I've been at the bucket end too and received a dowsing but I can't describe the joy when one feels the very strong suck of the calf's tongue on your fingers, followed by the first few swallows. You think you have won, but the experience has so delighted or surprised or frightened or nearly drowned the calf, that the head shoots up from the bucket and the calf gallops off in confusion about these mother figures and so the learning process has to go on. Soon the bucket is emptied in two or three minutes and its given a mighty head butt which you must be ready for, otherwise you go flying too.

I tried my hand at muck spreading. Frank would laugh at me when I vigorously thrust the fork into the manure where it stuck, and I couldn't lift it one inch. He taught me how to just pick up a shallow layer. Later I grew overconfident at this and pushed the fork through my heavy Dunlop Wellington boot, piercing my big toe. Floss was there helping Frank too, and she immediately took me back to the farmhouse and applied some sort of disinfectant. Tetanus injections weren't given in those days.

With all the fresh air, good nourishing food, exercise and the kindness of Mr Bingham, Floss and Frank, I was growing into a healthy strong girl who was happy and didn't always want to return home for school holidays.

On the 21st January 1943, during a daylight raid, Catford Central School in London was bombed, causing many injuries and fatalities. One of our teachers had only just returned to that building to teach, as numbers were now dwindling at Gilletts. It was with great shock and sadness that we heard Miss Knowelden had been killed. Spirits were very low as we pondered on the enormity of what had happened, and the suffering to so many families.

It was decided by the school governors for Smarden that so many children should not be together under one roof, as happened when the village children came up to Gilletts for their midday meal. So the village children would stay at their school, and we older Gillett girls would push their meals in a cart up to them, and help serve the meals to the children. This was done on a rota system. We all enjoyed helping in this way as the two schools had bonded very well over the years.

Life continued apace at Gilletts as we rehearsed for school plays and I was given a leading role as Rosalind, also shared by Eileen Tooke, in *As You Like It*. There were many lines to learn. I took the first part and Eileen the second.

At the farmhouse I would frequently be coping with my homework or learning my lines for the play by candlelight when Floss would come dashing into the living room with her fluttering fading candle, saying 'I won't be a minute', taking my candle and leaving me to continue my studies by the warmth and glow of the fire. I so well remember the smell of the logs and the intimacy of those fires that had burned down to a soft purr of flame.

Our school hours had to be extended to help cope with our commercial studies of shorthand, typewriting and bookkeeping. We were taking the Royal Society of Arts examinations. The subjects included English, French, German, Arithmetic, Geography, Shorthand, Typewriting and Bookkeeping, plus the Oxford School Certificate for nine of the very clever pupils. We all decided which exams we wanted to take, and there was no pressure put on us to sit exams beyond our capability. Each of us knew our responsibility in doing home study if we were to pass our exams, or at least do our very best. Our form teacher Miss Chaplin had become our friend as well as teacher, and we had great respect for her. She gave us her all, and we could discuss any of our worries or fears with her.

When cycling by one day, I noticed that there was some unusual activity in the Top Field at Ongley and that strange men, who from a distance didn't resemble any locals, were digging a deep narrow ditch.

I asked Floss, 'What's going on up Top Field?'

Floss answered, 'You must not tell anyone anything about this. Do you understand?' Her voice was very stern and her eyes large and appealing. I realised it must be something really important, and assured her that I wouldn't tell a soul.

Soon after, when returning home on my bike from school I turned off to go down Beech Lane when two army sentries stopped me, asking me why I was going down the lane.

I said, 'Because I live down there,' feeling somewhat bewildered. The sentries on duty outside Ibornden Park entrance were used to my comings and goings, why should I be stopped by what appeared to be a different platoon? However, on questioning me further, they were satisfied that I was an evacuee named Georgina Plumb billeted at East Ongley Farm. My chief guardian was Mr Bingham, under whom I was registered as he was the owner of the farm.

For several days the soldiers were there and I was waved through with a cheery 'Hello, off you go.'

I mentioned this to Mr Bingham, Floss and Frank, more as an observation than a question, as I didn't expect an explanation, and none was given.

It can now be told that the ditch I saw being dug was in fact a trench which ran across the Kentish fields to the English Channel and on the sea bed to France carrying petrol and was named PLUTO, meaning Pipe Line Under the Ocean. This was around the time of D-Day and when at home, on school holidays, placards were displayed everywhere with the words 'Careless Talk Costs Lives'. This became a common motto wherever one lived, and children as well as grown-ups learned to keep silent. I'm glad I did.

Parents of the Catford Central Girls billeted at Smarden and Bethersden were very lucky in the fact that Mrs Blundell had organized, very early on, a coach for them to visit their children every couple of months. Sometimes it was longer, as petrol became scarcer for public use. Parents of the Biddenden girls travelled individually the best way they could.

4

Life was never dull on the farm. Changing seasons brought different activities. The summers seemed to be very hot, which was a bonus for hay making. Mr Bingham never worked on a Sunday except for milking and feeding. It was the Lord's Day of rest and it would have been offensive to Him if Floss or I did any darning. It was nice to see him all scrubbed up in a clean shirt with an added stiff collar and in his best suit, ablutions having been done in a small galvanized bath, which he had previously taken upstairs to his bedroom. There were always a couple of large kettles on the kitchen range with hot water. Mr Bingham would then get his very tall spindly old bicycle out of the lodge and cycle to church, where he was sidesman.

But as the ministers for agriculture pressed harder for farms to increase their produce, work had to be done around the clock if necessary. Local labour helped each other out, especially if clouds were looming, when it would be a race to get the hay in. Even meals were put aside. They were glad to have a quick bite of a sandwich and a generous swigging of cold tea that Floss had hurriedly prepared and brought out for the men.

Mr Bingham wasn't able to go to church so often because of the Sunday work. When he was able to go one Sunday, he came back a very sad man. Floss told me someone else had taken his job as sidesman. He never attended a Sunday service again whilst I was there. I felt his sadness and knew what a good man he was at heart.

You need hay with some red clover in it and when it dries quickly, after being turned with the pitchfork, you see a slight greenness and colouring in the hay. Its wonderful aroma is never forgotten. I grew to love the earthy smells and the values of country life, and that passion has remained with me ever since and which I share with my country village friend Dorothy Watts.

One day in the small field, there were just Mr Bingham, Frank and myself. I was watching the hay being pitched up to Mr Bingham who was on the hay wagon behind the tractor, expertly stacking the hay into a safe load around him. Between Frank pitching up the hay he had to get on and off the tractor to move forward.

'Frank, let me drive the tractor forward for you, it would save a lot of time,' I said.

Frank readily agreed and showed me what to do. I waited for Frank's shout to proceed and took my foot off the clutch. There was an almighty jerk and a frightening shout from Mr Bingham who in no uncertain words told me to put a great distance between me and that tractor. The only blasphemy I'd ever heard Mr Bingham use before was 'Beggar it'. I'd nearly shot him off the top of a high load, only being saved by the fact he always leant heavily on the pitchfork well bedded down into the hay in the centre of the stack when moving. I hadn't realised that I was supposed to ease up slowly on the clutch!

Another summer, when stacking hay was going on up around The Buildings and labour was a bit short, I asked if I could go up on to the stack and help toss hay from where it was being pitched up. My friend Dorothy's father Mr Watts was building the stack expertly working on the corners first to keep it stable, and I tossed the hay in his direction. I soon mastered how to do that and thoroughly enjoyed doing it. At the end of the afternoon I was so thrilled to be praised by Mr Watts, who said I had pitched as good as any man.

As I was so very thirsty, not liking the taste of cold tea, I got on my bike and cycled to the nearest council houses half-way to Biddenden where a friend of mine was billeted, to ask if I could have a drink of water! How lovely it was too. Cold tea, ginger beer or milk never quenched my thirst as that water did then. There was tap water at Gilletts so I could enjoy that whilst at school.

As the very hot weather had lowered the small ponds again which were near to the farmhouse, all water was having to be carried by buckets from larger, deeper ponds further away. In the 15 minutes we were allowed to take a bath at Gilletts, none of us found it long enough to wash and dry our hair too. My hair had always been a nightmare to me – very thick, unruly curly 'mind of its own' hair. My mother had to use a wire hair brush with lots of gusto to try and get through the tangles. Once I was evacuated, it only got cut when I was home on school holidays. When I washed my hair at the farm, I used the small hand bowl in the sink and whatever piece of soap there was to hand, such as the large bar of green household soap. One day I must have put too much on and I just couldn't rinse it all out. I didn't like to use up too much water either, as it had to be carried such a long way. I dried my hair and it stuck out at all angles. It was a Sunday and I was going to church, so I pushed my school hat well down

49

on my head and off I went feeling rather fed up with myself. It soon passed as I realised what a stupid trifling little thing it was to worry about.

The mornings and late afternoons were lovely, walking through the fields to Biddenden and back as a change from cycling, in the hot hazy summer days. Then on to Smarden in the Buick with much banter amongst the girls and seeing a smile on Mr Small's face. I always put an extra spurt on through the fields to home, so that I could have a little time with Boxer if he wasn't out working. I would gently keep brushing the flies away from his eyes which he would close in contentment as I prattled on about school, or anything really. I'm not sure if he was particularly interested in hearing about all the various crops of fruit that we had helped Mr Wilmshurst grow at Gilletts, and that were being made into jam for our school canteen. He looked even sleepier when I told him of the huge harvest of potatoes we had helped dig up. Now carrots would have been more in his line, but Mr Wilmshurst managed those on his own, along with a lot of other vegetables which were gathered daily as needed.

With haying finished, soon it came to harvesting the golden fields of grain. Corn heads were snapped and shaken into the palm of the hand and a few seeds were chewed, followed usually by grunts of satisfaction. Local farmers and labourers got together to discuss and speculate which farm would have the use of the threshing machine first, and where it would go next. Near neighbours – meaning perhaps 2 or 3 miles away – would call on a late summer's evening and stay yarning and leg-pulling in the farm kitchen, helped on by a small glass of Mr Bingham's very special brew of cider. Their harvest relied so much on the weather and how quickly the grain could be safely gathered in.

50

I watched with great excitement when the tractor pulling a smallish machine behind started to cut the corn and throw it out in neatly bound sheaves. When several rounds of cutting had been done, and keeping well clear of tractor and cutting machine, Mr Bingham Floss and I and anyone else who happened to be about collected two sheaves of corn at a time and started to 'stook' by leaning the two sheaves together with the corn heads facing upwards and the other end splayed out to keep their balance. This was done with more pairs being added to make a stook of about eight sheaves. It was a very pleasing job, and once started you just kept going. It was only much later that you noticed what a state your arms and legs were in, as the stubble of the corn pierced the skin, scratching unmercifully, and left congealed droplets of blood in its wake.

When there was only a small circle of corn standing, work seemed to stop and I was surprised to see the men go to the sides of the field and return with their guns. I was warned to stay well back and not move. Frank started the tractor again and commenced to cut the remaining corn. I was taken aback to see rabbits running out in all directions from their fast-decreasing refuge, plus a few mice or voles. Shots were fired and in no time the dead rabbits were collected up and shared by the men. This was their bonus and a highlight for them. I really felt sorry for those poor terrified rabbits.

With ever-watchful eyes on the weather, local farmers and labourers gave help to the neighbouring farms where the threshing machine was working. They in turn would give a hand until all the corn crops were safely gathered in. Golden straw stacks were soon built in readiness to provide winter bedding for the animals, and mice were assured of a cosy place to call home.

51

Again there was much leg-pulling and teasing. Floss would take up sandwiches and cake for them and more cold tea. If I had helped to make the sandwiches Floss would tell me to put plenty of butter into the corners and edges. If she ever saw any sandwiches in the lane that had been thrown away (not hers I might add) she would pick them up and look inside.

'No wonder they threw them away – nothing much in them and all hard and dry round the edges,' she would say.

I learnt a lot from Floss, and her sayings and doings have always been with me. If she saw a dead bird on the ground she would look to see why it had died and was always upset if, when examining its crop, she felt it empty. She was a very compassionate person.

As threshing was a very dirty, dusty job I didn't care to stay around too long and many a time I was at school anyway. I did hear that some of the men would take a dip in any nearby pond at the end of the day in an attempt to rid themselves of some of the dust.

I very much liked the science lessons we had at school and we were learning about eyes. As we were encouraged to bring items of interest to class, one pupil, who was billeted with a butcher, left a small box on Miss Chaplin's desk for this lesson. Miss Chaplin picked up the box and lifted the lid. She quickly put her hand across her mouth, stretched out her arm and gesticulated for the box to be passed round the students. It was a large bullock's eye! Later we had to try stabbing it with a large pin to see how tough it was. I think Miss Chaplin could have been sick at what she saw. It had been so lovingly presented too!

This reminds me of the incident when Floss had a small bantam hen running free range round the garden. I made a pet of her and called her Pecky. I would peck about with her using a small stick in the soil around flower plants trying to find a tasty worm or grub. She would come close to me as I prodded about and one day she suddenly pecked my eye. I think it must have glinted in the light. Thankfully she had only caused a pink mark on the white of the eye and the pupil wasn't affected. The mark took a long time to disappear. I kept my head well out of her way after that.

Another problem occurred when I was badly scratched in-between the knuckles of the first and second finger of my right hand by a buck rabbit I was handling at school. I didn't take too much notice, but it did get progressively sore and one day, on cycling to Biddenden, it surprised me by bursting a lot of pus into my glove. On arriving at Gilletts I though I'd better mention it. Mrs Blundell sent me straight to the village doctor who bathed and dressed it and told me I must return the next day to have it looked at. As it would be a Saturday I had to cycle all the way from the farm to Smarden and back, a round trip of roughly 12 to 13 miles. I wasn't too happy about that. As there was little traffic on the roads when cycling to and fro from the farm to Biddenden, I often clutched a book whilst steering with the handlebars, and glanced down at intervals to learn my French verbs or similar homework.

We did have a bout of scabies at Gilletts which is very contagious, causing much itching especially between the fingers. Our hands and bodies were inspected regularly for any signs of scabies and were treated accordingly. Thankfully I never caught it, and the problem soon disappeared or rather it was cleared up.

When we were in our fifth form at Gilletts we had the chance to learn hockey. I don't know who had

53

supplied the equipment. We had plenty of hockey sticks but not enough shin pads, but that didn't deter us. With the help of the staff, who couldn't resist joining in when they had the chance, we enjoyed charging about in all directions until, at long last, we developed the skills of passing to one another and eventually scoring goals. I was scared stiff of one rather heavily built girl who literally charged down the field, and woe betide anyone who got in her way. Unfortunately, I was in the wrong place at the wrong time on one occasion, and received a mighty whack from her stick across my right unprotected shin. The dent in the bone has remained with me as a reminder. However, we couldn't wait for our chance to get lunches over and go off to play hockey, in addition to the hockey lessons that we had.

As I got older, I took it more in my stride going home for the school holidays, if things were reasonably quiet with regards to air raids. I was so very pleased if my dear brother managed to get home on leave too. We were even shy of each other when we first met. I no longer was 'As thin as a match stick with the wood scraped off,' as he used to say. He cut a fine figure in his RAF uniform, but he looked older than his years, no doubt due to being operational on Lancaster bombers which had taken its toll.

Our September holidays were always our longest and this is when hop picking starts on the farms, usually about the second week if the hops are large enough. To begin with I used to help Floss and pick into her bin. As I grew older I had a bin of my own and earned myself quite a bit of money. I used to go home for a week or a little longer and then Floss would write to say when they expected to start hop picking and I would return to the farm.

Hops were grown up strings attached to sturdy poles and the vines climbed their way along strings intertwining and making an avenue of plants. The leaves were heavily veined and coarse in texture, growing from sinewy coarse rasping stems. One had to be careful when walking, both to watch out and not be caught and be severely scratched on the face and arms by overhanging tangles of vines, or to be tripped and scored across the ankles by those partly hidden on the ground. The younger hop gardens always looked neat and tidy as the new plants were well trained, bore fewer but often longer and larger hops, with pale green petal-like shapes overlapping into a cone formation. As the plants matured they developed a mind of their own, although they had to be retrained up new strings each year after being cut short after harvesting the previous year. The hops grew into clusters from finger-like stems jutting from the vines.

A man would be employed to cut and pull the vines down and keep a regular supply going to each person picking. The bins into which the hops were picked were made from an oblong frame constructed from two lengths of wood approximately one and a half metres long, placed horizontally and attached to two wooden upstanding posts, criss-crossed at the top with the bottom splayed out acting as legs. Around the frame was nailed a canvas bag. It was divided down the middle by another section, and so two people would work independently side by side.

At East Ongley Farm, the hop fields were comparatively small, and they only employed their local friends and neighbours as compared to the large hop fields who employed gypsies and Londoners who lived and slept in tiny wooden huts, enjoying it as a holiday.

Prams, push chairs, stools, broken seats, sandwiches,

cake, cold bottles of drink, apples, old coats, apron sacks, anything and everything was brought to the fields to provide for the day's needs. Mornings often started cold with a nip in the air or a slight mist, but the days warmed up as the sun's rays sent out a pleasant warmth and danced on the different shades of green, mellowing the pickers into a happy crowd. Moods changed with the weather and you became lost in daydreams, at least I did, or got lost in nothingness, just happy in what I was doing. Small children sat on upturned boxes picking hops into old enamel bowls, baskets or boxes, and later played together when they'd had enough of picking contentedly, making up their own games.

It seemed to take ages even to cover the bottom of the bin and sometimes Floss would rapidly pick some vines into my bin as an encouragement. I noticed how instead of picking the hops singly, if there were bunches, Floss would quickly pick off the leaves and then, in one swoop, would strip all the hops into the bin. I started to do that too and it was satisfying to at last see I was getting results. Sometimes we would hear the sounds of distant aircraft which would bring our minds back to the ravages of war, and especially of my brother who was still flying in Lancasters as an engineer.

Mr Bingham would call out for us to prepare our bins for measuring at lunchtime. We had to look over the hops we had picked and remove as many leaves as possible which may have dropped in or attached to a hop in the picking. They would not be accepted if they had not been picked 'clean'. Mr Bingham came to each bin and measured the hops by scooping them from the bin in a bushel basket and then placing them into a large roomy sack called a poke. The number of bushels was recorded by Frank, or a neighbour, in a little book against each name.

Sandwiches were eaten with black tacky hands – this was the residue from the hops, and it left a slightly bitter taste. We enjoyed the food so much that no one seemed to take any notice. There was much friendship, banter and warmth amongst the hoppers. The afternoon proceeded much the same plus another measuring late afternoon. When all the fields of hops had been picked they looked strangely sad and dejected. Mr Bingham paid the pickers and I felt quite proud of myself to have earned a few pounds. Hop picking was a wonderful experience, one which many people from near and far looked forward to year after year.

Mr Bingham then began to stay days and nights up in the oast house as he had to keep a continual fire in the base of the round part of the oast house. The heat rises to dry the hops which are spread out onto a mesh above. The hops have a lovely smell which is hard to describe, and when they have been dried it is a wonderful aroma and so relaxing. When dry, Mr Bingham used a huge special rake to draw them back onto the floor of the oblong adjoining section of the oast house. They were pushed into a very long pocket sling canvas bag which dropped down into the ground floor below. Mr Bingham then pressed the hops tightly in the bag by means of a round heavy metal disc which he operated with a crank handle. This process was continued until the pockets were solidly packed to the brim and then they were tied up and stacked for collection. Frank helped Mr Bingham too, as the work was continuous with the need to get all the harvested hops dried and pressed.

Floss suggested that we should both go and spend a night up in the oast house, as she hadn't done that for many a year and it would be a first for me. We took pillows and light blankets and laid them on the first floor well away from the hot air rising into the drying area. Mr Bingham had a permanent wooden bunk in a corner screened off by heavy sacks. We were soon asleep with the heavy aroma of hops born on the warm air surrounding us. I was awoken sometime later from my sleep by loud scratching noises and shuffling scraping thumps, many of which were coming from the staircase leading up from the ground floor.

Floss stirred too and whispered, 'Mice and rats.' She pulled the blankets tightly in around her and advised me to do so too. Not long ago she had been really spooked by a mouse which had got into the dairy room at the farm house and tried to run up her leg in its panic to escape. Her squeals had brought Frank running to her rescue, though he couldn't help laughing. So we both tried to ignore the antics of our night friends and go back to sleep. Somehow it wasn't the same then, and we were glad when morning came, but it was an experience.

I did go on to pick for a further week one year when Ongley's picking had completed and another farm was short of pickers. Floss asked if I would like to go to give a hand – she had too much work around the farm and house to catch up on as only the bare essentials could be done during busy hopping season. I worked alongside a lot of gypsies who were very pleasant, but I had a job to understand their lingo. A very handsome lad named Mushy was our vine puller and he could be heard singing as he went about his work. Later he was never seen or heard singing anywhere. One of the gypsy girls said that he had been banished from their midst as he had got a girl into trouble.

Frank grew lovely vegetables and I watched how

Floss cut runner beans into thicker pieces than she would normally do when cooking them straight from the garden, layering them in a big stone crock with handfuls of coarse salt. A few days later more would be added and in time the juice from the beans with the salt made a brine, which preserved the beans for months and were so useful in the winter. They were well rinsed before going into the saucepan and no further salt was added. Nothing could beat fresh runner beans, but they made a good vegetable in bad weather when all was frozen to the ground. I was fascinated too how Frank twisted and placed his large fat round golden onions onto long strings hanging their heavy weights from beams to complete their drying.

Soon I was saying, 'Frank, can I have a go?'

'Of course you can,' he'd willingly reply, with a shuffle of his cap, which seldom was removed until evening when it exposed a very pale forehead against a weather-tanned face.

I really liked the job of stringing onions. Harvesting acorns was a pleasant and useful pastime too, because although they were bad for cattle, they were fed to pigs. All my senses were very alert to nature as I foraged about under the big oak trees, admiring the enormous strength of their trunks and branches.

The time was drawing near when many of us would be leaving as we were approaching 16 years of age. We had all become close friends, as one big family, and the thought of leaving was hard to comprehend. We talked about the type of jobs we would be seeking – there were plenty of them about as so many people were serving in the various armed forces. We promised to keep in touch with each other as we weren't too many miles apart where we lived on the outskirts of southeast London. Mrs Blundell had been a wonderful

59

headmistress and her husband, Mr Blundell, was a great support to both her and the girls, in helping make and mend articles requiring his handicraft skills which he also taught to local schools. We were also fond of Miss Chaplin, who was always there for us and had had to teach us many extra subjects, which she had to learn quickly in advance. We remembered other teachers fondly too who were at Gilletts, and had shaped our lives, thinking of Miss Patterson, Miss Curdy, Miss Atkinson, Miss Salvadori and Miss Knowelden.

My thoughts turned to the farm and Floss, Frank and Mr Bingham. Perhaps I could stay there. I'd get a job and would be able to pay for my keep, instead of the government paying a subsidy for me as an evacuee. But what sort of job could I hope to get in the village to make the most of the commercial skills I'd learned? My father had spoken of getting me into the printing trade, as he belonged to their trade union in London and had done so for many years. I was expected to go home. All my close friends of the fifth form, except a few who were carrying on for a further year, taking more exams in order to go into the teaching profession, were returning. I really didn't want to go. I would miss their friendship, but most of all I would miss Floss, Frank and Mr Bingham who had given me a solid home life. 'Whatever happens I'll come back as often as I can and I'll write too, my heart will always be here and there's Boxer, he will miss me, I must come back. Perhaps, when I'm 18 years old, I'll join the Land Army and see if I can get posted to Biddenden and lodge at East Ongley, that's what I'll do.' These were my thoughts.

One day I went off on my bike as I often used to do, just cycling here, there and everywhere as most signposts had been removed completely. Thankfully, I always managed to find my way back to the farm. I came across several fields planted with small little fir trees. There were hundreds and hundreds of them. I dropped my bike on the grass verge and picked out a really nice shaped one and pulled it gently out of the ground. Stepping back onto my bike I was able to hold both the handlebar and the small fir tree in my left hand. I thought Floss would like the tree, and cycled back as pleased as anything. I'd never seen such a choice of fir trees.

I was coming up the path when Floss looked out of the back door and said with a startled, horrified look on her face, 'Where did you get that'? Pointing to the fir tree.

'There were fields with lots of them,' I said with some surprise.

'Did anyone see you?' Floss asked with some urgency.

'I don't know. I don't think so,' I said, feeling bewildered.

'Don't you ever do that again. I just hope no one saw you. Those fields most certainly were planted by the Forestry Commission and it would be considered as stealing,' she said.

'Oh dear,' I thought, 'How was I to know?' I hadn't meant to do wrong, but it was another lesson learned.

Two or three days later I was surprised to see that the little fir tree had been planted in the garden, near to the road and close to the gate leading to the back door. Not another word was said about it.

All too soon, Easter school holidays approached and Mrs Blundell handed the girls, who were leaving, their school testimonials. Those last days were a blur except I remember going off on my own to walk around the Gilletts garden, the paddock and the place where we had played hockey and thinking how I was going to miss it all. I hurried back to the house, there were things to do. Up the back stairs and down the main staircase – shall I go just once up the main staircase and down the back staircase?

I bought a small tin of furniture polish in the village and, after packing up my belongings at the farm, I cleaned and polished my bedroom. My mother came to help me with my extra luggage and Floss gave a hand carrying some too, as we walked the 2½ miles round the road to Biddenden to catch the bus to Maidstone and eventually home.

I can find no words to express how I felt on that journey, but have dreamt of it many times.

EPILOGUE

On the 27th April 1944 I started work as a trainee wages clerk with the Amalgamated Press in London. I was also trained as a telephonist by the GPO to help cover the firm's switchboard in the event of staff being absent due to bombing. Doodle bugs were prevalent at the time.

My brother Ivon was killed in May 1944 over France. Our remaining Gilletts school girls were re-evacuated to Cornwall.

Floss and Frank had a son named John a year after I had returned home.

Two of my Catford Central friends from Gilletts came to work for the Amalgamated Press on the request of the office manager.

I spent many holidays back at the farm. Due to the tragedy of my brother's death I felt unable to leave my mother and pursue the idea of joining the Women's Land Army.

Dorothy Watts came to visit us frequently and our friendship flourished. I became a Scout Cub mistress and met a Rover Scout named Gordon Hughes who was to become my husband in 1950. About the same time Dorothy Watts met a local Smarden lad called Gordon, who became her husband a few months after our wedding. His surname was Hughes. We both had two sons. We are still close friends and share the same interests. Many harvest times have seen us back on the farm with Gordon driving the tractor and assisting on the combine harvester. In 1958 we moved from London to a bungalow in Willesborough, Ashford, Kent, close to my schoolfriend Brenda who married the son of the family she was billeted with in Bethersden. Several girls have returned to those areas. We are all very much in touch with each other, through a network spreading far and wide. We had forged a special bond, strengthened by reunions.

Mr Bingham died, and in later years Floss and Frank retired to a more peaceful way of life, enjoying their house and garden near Tenterden, Kent. Both have since died.

I am still in touch with their son John and his wife. John did not go into farming but happily works for himself in agriculture.

The fir tree has now grown big in the front garden of the farm house. The fact that it still remains there tells its own story. I could never have had a better billet or such lovely people as my guardians, who will never be forgotten, and to whom I owe so much.